The Voice After

LAUREN FOSTER

To request permissions or bulk orders, contact the author at:
Laurenfosterbook@gmail.com

Published By Writing in Faith
IAmWritingInFaith.com

Cover Design & Interior Design By: Faiza Mehboob
Contact : zunirffm@gmail.com

Lauren Foster (Text)

ISBN 13: 978-1-7353541-9-4

The Voice After

Oh.

                                                    The stinging sensation.

The immaculate vibrations.

                                                    The fear of it all.

My mind says yes.

                                                    But my body is sluggish.

The words coming out of your mouth are just rubbish.

                                        Oh, the fear of it all.
                                        Oh, the cheers are too tall.

Oh?
How so?
How can you satisfy the body of a woman?
How can you be so sure my body is woman ...enough?
How can you be so sure?

Oh.

                                                    The shrill of it all.

                                                                Oh.

The thrill of it all.

                                                                Oh.

How come it's always

                                                    The fear of it all.

It's always **the voice after**
It always lingers
Just when you reach **the final chapter**
It lathers between your fingers

Just when your heart enables **a hearty laughter**
It thinks you've forgotten to listen
In case you thought **all you hold dear doesn't matter**
It causes you to convulse and think different
It will be heard
It will not be faint
It will demand to be observed
It will cause you to paint, the colors of the wind
When and where it all began
It began, with a simple question
Have you forgotten?

Have you forgotten who you **are**?
Have you forgotten the meaning of a star?
Have you forgotten the line in your heart?
Have you forgotten that you are **lost**?
Have you forgotten that you have thoughts?
Have you forgotten that you can be bought?
Have you forgotten you can only wear **sheer**?
Have you forgotten that weakness is shown through tears?
Have you forgotten that you have fears?
Did you forget that fears can turn into cheers?

The wedding bell cheers
The champagne pops open our ears
The couple smiles
Why am I still single?
The couple dances a couple of dances
Everyone cheers

Why do I feel so alone?
The bride throws the bouquet
An acquaintance catches
Feelings?
Lust?
The groom sits the bride in a chair and slips off her garter belt with his teeth
Cheers enveloped the room like an awkward spirit

It doesn't have to be lonely being alone
But **lonesome** is a fearsome beast with a yearning for a burning embrace
Tears trickle down your face as you realize no one is coming to the party
No one wants to be a nobody
No one wants to have somebody
They're too busy trying to move faster than their mind
They're too busy trying to find the meaning to the life
There is no meaning

Their valid reason is not valid enough
Someone will call you on your bluff
And find out you are just as lonely as one can get
Let's not forget that you are lonely

You are **hurting**
You are hurting from the inside
The line in your heart has been disabled to start
You are hurting
You are in pain
This is as much pain as pain can get

Oh. The **fear** of it all.

One can try to escape
One can elaborate a master plan
Fool-proof
Little did you know the fool was you
You tried to escape
but **love is an electric eel**; it shocked you and created electric veins
And you learned how to feel
You learned how to give them the pencil to open the seal
Little did you know they would write all over you
You learned how to stop cutting onions and put the knife on the shelf
Little did you know that knife, in the wrong hands, could stab and deteriorate your
mental health
It hurts
It will always hurt

You've forgotten you have thoughts
Thoughts that are so complex yet so simple
Thoughts that can be so real yet so imaginary
Inception
Pure creation
Utter illusion
Limbo
How low can you go?
How low can you feel?
Nothing you're feeling is real
We are all particles of dust with bones
We are all bones that will rust into dust
We will all fall into ruts and we will get stuck
Ladders won't matter
Stairs won't care

Stairs   Stairs
    Will   Be
        Always   Always
            Be   Will
                Stairs
            Will   Be
        Always   Always
    Be   Will
Stairs   Stairs

You will just stand there
There will always be stairs

                                              Climb
                                          To
                                      You
                                  For
                          Stairs
                      Be
              Always
          Will
    There

oh.
        oh.
            oh.

                    The song of the weary.
oh.
        oh.
            oh.
                    The dance of the teary-eyed.
                    The chance of a merry ride.

It's always **the voice after**.

oh.
    oh.
      ...oh.

The voice after **a disaster** usually comes before **the laughter**.

And the laughter is the best part
Only crying tears of joy and only slouching because you're used to boulders
But when you look to the left at all you left behind
You see shoulders by your side
And the voice after is thrown like a dart
Pinning down your final inhibition to the board
And all the fight won't be in vain
Because the vile memories you would hoard caused you pain
And that pain helped you grow

Pain helps you grow
With every rose, there are thorns
And those thorns have stayed with you since the day you were born
But pain will help you grow

Oh, **the thrill** of it all.

Pricked by renowned beauty
Hiding underneath the "skin deep"
is something deeper than "skin deep"

The pain that helped you grow.

The pain has just become tolerable
The pain has just eased off so you can at least stand
You can at least get out of bed
You can at least rub the crown of your head
When your tongue rejuvenates, it doesn't taste like **dry dread**
It doesn't infect your mind with laziness
For the first time in what might've felt like a lifetime
You have energy

Adrenaline...

Oh the fear of it all...

No one can fathom adrenaline until you're trying to say a mantra...
In for 4, out for 8
Keep your cool, now you're great
...while slowing your breath...
In for 4, out for 8
...when you're not even under arrest...
When you see the blue lights
And your life seems to fly faster than light
And all can be covered and be swept in the middle of the night
And all the Halloween witches can see their brooms stolen
And all of the color melt into hot lava of anxiety
Maybe tonight I am The Chosen
The cop asked me for my license and registration
Yet he pulled his gun out with no hesitation
And another black soul has been betrayed by this nation
I am The Chosen

In for 4, out for 8
Keep your cool, now you're great
In for 4, out for 8
In for 4, out for 8
In for 4, out for 8

In and out
Keep them out
Keep them out of the head
Keep them out of the mind
They go on nonstop all night
They tie you up and cover up the light
They hate not being right
They hate being wrong
As long as there is a shrill tune they sing in their song
All that is right is wrong
Have you ever **fought a demon?**
Have you ever **sought treason?**
Have you ever **thought about the seasons?**

Seasons of change
Seasons in which you have molded into anew
Seasons in which expose a new you
Becoming a winner after falling into the heat of summer and yet springing into
new life
New Renown
The old mirror is broken now
New Flowers
You have stared in the mirror for hours
Yes

This. Is. You.

You have flourished
You have been furnished
You have been tortured long enough
Do you believe in happiness?
The demons fled as soon as your eyes duplicated the color of the sun
The angels flew in and untied you from the unprecedented pedestal you fed your
soul upon
Look upon the skies and wonder why

The thrill of it all killed it all

The breaths are not working
The chest is still jerking
Why won't you calm down?
It's not that I won't, it's that I can't
Why do you always turn around?
Because there are shadows threatening to take my earthly position
Trying to transmit the transitions to tasting the tar
It can't possibly be that hard

It can't possibly be that hard

It can't possibly be that hard   *It can't possibly be that hard*

It can't possibly be that hard

9

It Can''t Possibly It Can''t Possibly Be That Hard Be That Hard

Right?

Words speak louder than sound
Same way as actions speak louder than words
The same way you touch the ground
Is the same way you can get hurt

Oh, the shrill of it all.

The voice after every ladder has shattered and there's no way to climb
It'd be easier to kick rocks and call this win a loss, but that would be a waste of time
Why be a waste of time?
Why be a waste of space?
Why not be treated as a celestial being?
You are worth fighting for
You can't want to die anymore
Death is a sweet release after completing your purpose
And you are not done yet
You do not hold your breath
Dragonsssssss breath
You must fight until nothing is left
Fight, fight, win!

Where would we be if Martin Luther King didn't dream?
Fight!
Where would we be if Malcolm X didn't instill by any means necessary?
Fight!
Where would we be if Claudette Colvin and Rosa Parks didn't refuse their seats
on the bus?
Fight!
Where would we be if Sam Cooke didn't sing "A Change Gonna Come?"
Fight!
Where would we be if Madame CJ Walker didn't learn and study the magic of
black hair?
Fight!
Where would we be if T'Challa didn't rise from the dead and fight for Wakanda?
Fight! Fight! Win!

We deserve to fight
We do nothing more but fight
We raise our spirits after we've lost in a fight
We raise our fists and continue to fight
Because we cannot stop the fight
Our melanin is telling them to shoot
Reboot and try again
The color of our skin is not free ammunition
It is simply pigmentation
We deserve to live bravely in this nation
Without the anticipation of not making it back to the celebration
We deserve liberation

Oh, the shrill of it all.

We deserve liberation from the chains
Shackled by tackled plays
Wanting, yearning for a touchdown on the torched ground when no sound is
around
Listen, to the echo
Listen, and say hello
You will hear a voice back
The voice after
Is usually after a chill escapes the rafters
And you're frozen shut
There is no magic, no ice to let it go
Unless…

You learn to let go
You learn to expose yourself out of your comfort zone
You learn to answer the phone
They've been calling all night
You learn that blankets eventually have to get washed
You learn that in order to be a french fry, you must be squashed
You learn to love you for you
And nothing about that is wrong; it's right
You learn, you grow, you become human
You learn to let it go

So what now?
You don't think you deserve love?
You think you are unworthy of love?
Why must you think this way, Love?
Love is a circus act that requires a juggle
Love is what enters a dark room in the midst of a struggle

Love is indeed a jump for the doves
Are you a dove, Love?
Is this just a gateway to Hate, Love?
Your mortal enemy?

Oh. The cheers were too tall.

Hate, why do you sit tall on your throne filled with lost souls?
Souls that have lost direction and veer into your reflection
Watch as they mold into your complexion
Infrared, infuriated, in drooling dread, instigated
It's all to your liking, **Hate**.
This is why you go hiking on the earth and soil on all you have soiled
You crave for me to overheat and burst into flames when I've been boiled
You twist your fingers in my hair but not for it to be coiled
You slip your serpents down each of my strands
I stumble when I stand
I have turned into Medusa
Could you be any more sinister, **Hate**?
Aren't you a dove, Love?
Love, as small as an infant, swoops in and attacks
Of course, **Hate** fights back with every punch and every slap
But all **Love** does is extend its hand for **Hate** to clap
Make amends
Become one unit
A vigilante
LoveHate.

SadMad. BitterSweet. AngerFear. SadnessViolence. HappySad.

Mixed Feelings, Mixed Emotions

13

Why are we trapped at the seafloor of a fixed ocean?
Listening to river flows as our shivering toes wave in a bliss motion
Almost hearing this distant locomotive of something that often goes unnoticed

Mixed Feelings, Mixed Emotions

Shea butter and cocoa butter lotion
A natural scent, a natural devotion
Some think we conjure up a potion
Why the sun lands on us at even proportion
Why do they say we're glitched, distorted
We listen for the locomotive

Mixed Feelings, Mixed Emotions

Pills and potions
It tastes like poison
But we too busy posin'
Not listening to the locomotive
The voice after a party is much safer than sorry
Because nobody wants an apology for the mixed feeling
Of nothing
Of everything
You are headed for a downward spiral
A downward maze
A download of info entitled **No Escape: The Algorithm**
As another song plays yet has the same rhythm
The room is filled with red lights
Before it goes to black.

Oh.

                                        The immaculate vibrations.

The stinging sensations.

                              Can my body be woman enough?

My body is sluggish, I am tired.

            I have fought for my body in hotel lobbies with hotel lobbyists.

            Check in, check out, check in, check out

Room service, there are no towels about
There is nothing to wipe it...all

                  Oh! The shrill of it all. Oh! The thrill of it all. Oh! The hills were
too tall.

Tell me.

                              Is it time to bawl or brawl at the ball?

Neither? Both?

Neither, because you have fought for a long time
There is no reason why you shouldn't relax
With **cucumbers** in and on your eyes
It is okay to let go
It is okay to go with the flow
Both, because you have fought for a long time

And never got your poetic justice
You never found your freedom
Your paradise
Inhale, exhale
Now you are in paradise

Palm trees configured into a spiritual being
The ocean creates lines with sighs of spiritual release
The sand welcomes your toes into foreign territory
Inhale, exhale
I am in paradise
Storms still weather, but I've become better
At finding peace
The voice after a disaster seems to go by faster
When you find peace
Cucumbers in and on your eyes as the skies turn to an orange-pink mix
And you're left with nothing else but breaths
Inhale, exhale
And I'm left with nothing else but breaths
Inhale, exhale

Empty
Hollow
Sorrow
Numb
Follow the sound of laughter despite the might of the hue of blue
Can't you see the true colors?
Can I see the true color?
The voice after all the thoughts shatter is nothing but stillness
Nothing but the realness of how deep the deep end is
Sinking deeper, lower into a depressive state
Reliving the days of free real estate
Where will It live?
When will It leave?

I guess it's up to me
All the world's burdens placed on small shoulders
Cracked, chipped, gnawed, open skin raw
Rocks and boulders
I guess it's all up to me
I was born older before I was born young
I was already underground before I dug
I was being smothered before I knew it was a hug
And yet I was still breathing even with the puncture in my lung
When all is said and all is done

You are in paradise.

You are the beach.

You are the waves.

You screech like seagulls

A reminder that sunset is on the way.

Are you okay?

A reminder that night approaches.

You howl at the moon.

Your eyes alter and you lose your focus.

All while being in your room.

Is everything okay?
Are you okay?
Is everything okay?
Why aren't you okay?
Be okay.

Okay?

Now, are you okay?
Please be okay
Now, is everything okay?
Why did no one check if she was okay?

Okay?

oh.

oh.

...oh.

What killed it all
Was the fear crawling down the walls
And the shrill that disturbed the call
It was all too tall
It was all too small
To be the cheers we found after being mauled

Oh, the thrill of it all.

Reincarnation
A new leaf, a new life
A child
A fresh start
A burning desire to make things better
To make some changes
Holding on tight to the first of many
The First of the Future

So, why **Baby Blue?**

Looking in the deep blue of Baby's eyes
Living life in little blue lies
Hiding the deep blue rivers inside
Falling into the demise of **Baby Blues**
How do you know that my body is woman enough?
How do you know that I am enough?
How do I provide the ideal life for a human identical to me?

Hide behind spite?
Hide behind disapproval?
Disappointment?
Appointments and appointments with imaginary therapists and therapists
Looking for an unreal diagnosis
The Baby is Blue
Revert to drugs to fill the void of hugs
The Baby is Blue

The baby has sprouted its wings out of the shell of metamorphosis
But at the end of the day
Butterflies are just bugs
If only they had dug deeper

The Baby is Blue.

The Baby is trying to radiate your hue,

But The Poor Baby was, is, and will still be blue

The Poor Baby has turned Blue.

27 Club.

His life has left his body.

His face is now blue.

Even though butterflies are still bugs,

Even though they only live for a week,

Butterflies stay butterflies.

The Baby became a Blue Butterfly.

Guilt holds and serenades you warm in discomfort
As he ascends to Heaven, there go the 7 stages
Variants of coping mechanisms
Variety of ways to silence **The Voice**

The voice after my cousin's funeral was quiet
My head was empty
Voided
Oh, the fear of it all...
The fear of silence
The fear of the quiet
Only hearing the sounds of pings from **The Algorithm**

Oh, the shrill of it all...

Mother, father
Souls connected whether by chance or love
Tied together after an intimate night
The night it all happened
The voice after the wine-and-dine induced laughter usually comes from a place called the heart
The smiles cracked the mouth and the teeth shown are sharp
Love, the electric eel, the mermaid, will take a bite out of you
And will leave a bulging scar
Since Love makes you feel like you are drowning
Drowning under miscommunications
Under the arguments
Under sore throats as the water adds more to the throat
Love drowns
Love makes you feel like drowning
Drowning into the tears into pillows
Drowning into the fear of the willow bark after dark
Can anything heal the pain?
Love, after all, drowns

But then you float

The disagreements, the stubbornness
Two bulls butting heads in the same stable, same rodeo, comes to a halt
The final grain of salt taps the sand mound inside the hourglass
This too shall pass
Mother, father
You can learn to love again
Father, you can love again
Mother, you can finally love
It could be **the night it all happens**

...and then silence...

After entering the Algorithm
You hear the pings
Or noises in general
You hear how its calculated computer system brings
Temporary emotions
Permanent commotions
Provocative locomotives having *loco* motives destined to crash at the end of the line
But
There's a fine line between being finished and coming to the end

Oh, the thrill of it all.

Do you believe you can throw in the towel while wiping your face?
Do you believe you can both move and stay in place?
Do you believe you can have a sweet and sour taste?

The answer is yes.

Because deep down, you don't want to finish before seeing the end

You don't want to end before reaching the finish line

...before seeing the outcome from all your income...

The voice after my cousin's funeral was quiet
Silence
Wondering how a 4-year-old will hear all these voices
After

After realizing that growing up is not just time elapsing
It is mindset
After realizing that the world is too big to try and keep grasping
It is mindset
It is a sunset shimmering on a lonesome beach
Tracks on the shore but near the water

Because love drowns

And now you start hearing the sounds
Loud peace
Rambunctious peace
Haunting peace
Peace that seems too good to be true
What do you do?
Do you swallow into this vacuum?
Do you see deranged infrared rays and waves as you wave your hand?
Standing on the fact that silence kills

Love drowns

...sinks...

You have tasted wicked flesh
You have torn into forbidden mesh
How are you so sure I am woman enough?
How are you so sure my body is the one to love?
All its scars and all its scratches
How you have no reaction
How you remain unfazed
How you remain unscathed from the flames of my disastrous mind
How you tend to find the calm in the storm
How you tend to always keep me warm
Sheltered in the best way possible

The voice after I heard him whisper my name
It calmed me
The lonesome beach has washed someone ashore
Someone who adores me more
Mirrors have been abject insecurities
Something he washes away
Even when the waves do their bidding
He keeps my heart skipping beats
He keeps me calm
The voice after all the calamity
Is calm

Lauren Foster

And yet...

      And yet...

            And yet...

                  And yet...

                        And yet...

                  And yet...

...and yet...

A lying, conniving dweller feasts on the remnants of a broken heart
The voice after a lying, deceiving craft maker officially perfected their perfect craft
Manipulation
Overwhelming thoughts succumb you in the dead of night
Causing you to wander the lonesome streets
The wet concrete from a mysterious force
Either from the rain or tears
Next thing you know you're drowning

Love sinks and love drowns
And you are sunken without sound

You are underwater
Fighting for your life
Not able to see the light of the past life
Only the bottom of the ocean
The toward to your forever life
But you see a light
Yet your eyes have become a lifeless lie
Will there be another side?
Is this the entrance to the other side?
Somehow, someway, will we collide?
You see a hand reaching yet you can't seem to extend
Is this the end?

No.

Love is beauty and love is kind
Love is sacred and scary to find

Life comes back into your lungs
You resuscitate as you forcibly grab that reaching hand
With so much motion in little time, you are back on the surface
You are back to life
Although love drowns, it also saves
It brings you back to life
It reminds you of the joys in life
It hinders all the strife that would splice like a thousand knives

Lauren Foster

And yet…

      And yet…

            And yet…

                And yet…

                    And yet…

              And yet…

…and yet…

Love forces you to doubt yourself
Love forces you to out yourself
Love forces you to collect yourself
Love forces you to reject yourself
Love forces, love drowns, love sinks
Love blends and mixes with all of the colors
Love blends and mixes well with others
LoveHate, the vigilante
Screeching for attention like a wild banshee

And yet...

        And yet...

                And yet...

                        And yet...

                            And yet...

                    And yet...

...and yet...

When its tasks are done
The vigilante splits apart
Reclaiming their two separate hearts
And then...
Hate evaporates
And Love accepts you
You in your full form
This should be the new norm
A formality without causality and a chance to get out of uniform
A chance to deform
Shed the sheer into pure light
A fairy instead of a sprite despite all you've held with your might

        Oh. The cheer in it all!

Lauren Foster

Does it tender you?
Does it render to your needs?
Does it feed you wishes and promises?
Does it fill your empty stomach?
Does it feel good?

Does it hold you?
Does it pluck hidden gold in you?
Is it true you performed those astonished sonnets?
Did it fill your empty stomach?
Did you sing how Love would?
Hate stands in the shadow, nodding with acknowledgment
LoveHate

Two souls sworn as enemies, becoming a vigilante, and becoming
Human

I wish he knew that he was human
I wish he knew that despite my silence he could converse with me
I wish he knew that he was broken
I wish he knew that his insight wouldn't have reversed me
It would've made me look up to him
It would've made me look forward to family gatherings on my mom's side
It would take away this image in my head
I don't think I could've been there when they pronounced him dead
I don't think I could've been there when my uncle found him dead
My vivid imagery already envisioned it in my head
What would've happened if he was laying in bed?

And all that was swirling in his head was dreams and hugs and all
Not drugs laced with fentanyl
I wonder what would've happened if we had that infamous "favorite cousin"
relationship
I wonder if LoveHate infected him, conflicted him
I wonder if the vigilante made him feel like he did it
Made him both love and hate what he was doing
What he had become
Most people thought that my silence was equivalent to naivety
But I always listened
It lurks, **the voice after**
I wonder if he knew he was trapped in a simulated system meant to degrade him
I wonder if he knew all he could have done with his greatness
I wonder if he knew his black boy joy caused irritable coy noise to those who
crave culture
Those who cave in to their spirit animal: vultures
Saving the bones for last as they digest the melanin
They yell in Hell because they can tell what is not theirs
I wonder if he knew it was not theirs
I wonder if he knew even black boys can cave into vultures
It lurks, **The Voice After**
I wonder if he knew more than he let on
I wonder if he knew his now 7-year-old son at first did not want to go to Heaven
I wonder if he knew he would fly away at 27
I wonder if he knew he turned into a blue butterfly
I wonder if he knew before then he was a slug
I wonder if he knew deep within, he craved hugs
I wonder if he knew his mother has become a different person who's in between
the 5th and 6th stage
I wonder if he knew his father is busier than ever and yet is the one who found him
I wonder if he knew his spirit still lurks in the house
It lurks, **the Voice after**
Was he aware that he was blue?
Baby Blue.

A whole episode of Love, Death, and Robots
Each anthropological episode has something to do with love, death, and robots
We are all Love, Death, and Robots
Stuck
Out of luck
Screaming, yelling, what the f-
I think that's enough
We all have experienced Love, Death, and Robots
Every episode
Every chapter
Every click
Every time

 Oh.

You told me to turn the TV on.

Oh.

You told me to get trapped in their world.

Oh.

You told me I would love to be trapped in this world.

Truth is?

You told the truth

How uncouth would it be of me to say I hate reality?
I hate The Algorithm
I hate being in a simulation in some mad scientist's equation to answer the riddle
of creation
This nation, this world
What a wonderful world
What a traversing world
How uncouth would it be of me to say

.oh.

How womanly can I be for you to yell
To tell everyone the wrongs in my body
That I am nobody
I am somebody
I am some...body
Floating with passion
Gloating with old-fashioned vomit
I am disgusting
Slimy tongues speaking familiar languages I disengage
I disregard
What comes from a bottomless heart
I'm starting to think I'm not just sluggish

I am the rubbish words your lips pressed to me
I am the mind, body, and soul of this traversing world
Of my traversing world
Why in the world would anyone want to traverse
It lurks, **The Voice After**
It all ended in a disaster

And then came the finale

The true question of when we all fall asleep, where do we go
The true question of what happens
The true question is if you will see **Blue Butterflies**
The answer?

The true question is whether or not we are ready for it to be permanent
When most, if not all of our lives, have been compiled into short-term temporaries
The true question is if you can see **Blue Butterflies Fly So High**
The answer?

Questions on top of questions to distract us from reflections
They say He will show you your life, your reflection
The true question is if we will get acceptance or rejection
The answer?

Oh, the shrill of it all

No Escape: The Algorithm

It's never really over until you're over

It's never really over until you're over

It's never really over until you're over

It's never really over until you're over

Is It Over Yet?

Is It Over Yet?

Is It Over Yet?

34

Lauren Foster

Please...

Please...

Let It Be Over
Over...over...
Over...over...

And yet...

And yet...

And yet...

And yet...

And yet...

And yet...

...and yet...

The thrill of it all was never a thrill at all.

Oh

Oh

Oh

The Finale...

Permanent...

Lock the door to an empty house full of furnishings...

Here's The End

Cradle yourself in all the newfound love you've found in others-

And yourself...

Keep those cucumbers on your eyes
Embedded melanin in a bed to become laminated
Forever a memory, forever a purpose
You are hopeless
You are not hopeless
Remoteness
Control your own life
Give up
Don't give up

Oh! Oh! Oh!

The Voice After...

Is the voice quiet now?
Will the voice ever be quiet?
Is the voice still loud?

Oh. The thrill of it all

Oh, the fear of it all.

Oh, the cheers are too tall.

Oh.

It's always **the voice after**
It always lingers
Just when you reach **the beginning chapter**
You caress it with your fingers
Just when you enable **the hearty laughter**
It thinks you've disobeyed because you forgot to listen
In case you forgot **all you hold dear matters**
It causes you to grow numb and become indifferent
It will be heard
It will not be faint
It will demand to be observed
It will cause you to paint footprints and fingerprints on walls
Call after call and it all begins
It begins... with a simple question
Have you forgotten?

Will we be forgotten?
Will they ignore?

Oh...

      Oh...

            Oh...

The voice after is the voice before.

www.ingramcontent.com/pod-product-compliance
Lightning Source LLC
Chambersburg PA
CBHW041811040426
42449CB00004B/146